TO THE MIGHTY:

FROM:

DATE:

A LETTER TO PARENTS

I am beyond excited to share this series with you! As a mother, I fully understand the need for a more precise understanding of biblical principles. Our children do not need a watered down version of The Bible - they are brilliant, unaffected by doubt, and not jaded. During childhood is the time to begin to instill principles that will impact them for the rest of their lives. Through the story of Esther they will learn that God has empowered them to live a victorious life, even in the face of adversity; that God has chosen them for such a time as this.

ABOUT THE MIGHTY SERIES

The Mighty Series is a compilation of children's books taken directly from the Word of God without the side of political correctness. There isn't a junior Holy Spirit for kids; they can walk in the fullness of their calling and destiny right now. The Bible says in Joel 2:28, "Your sons and daughters will prophecy..." The Bible is filled with promises for our children! As you read these books to them, know that you are ministering to their spirits, and building them up to be everything God has called them to be!

BASED ON THE TRUE BIBLICAL
STORY FOUND IN THE BOOK OF

ESTHER

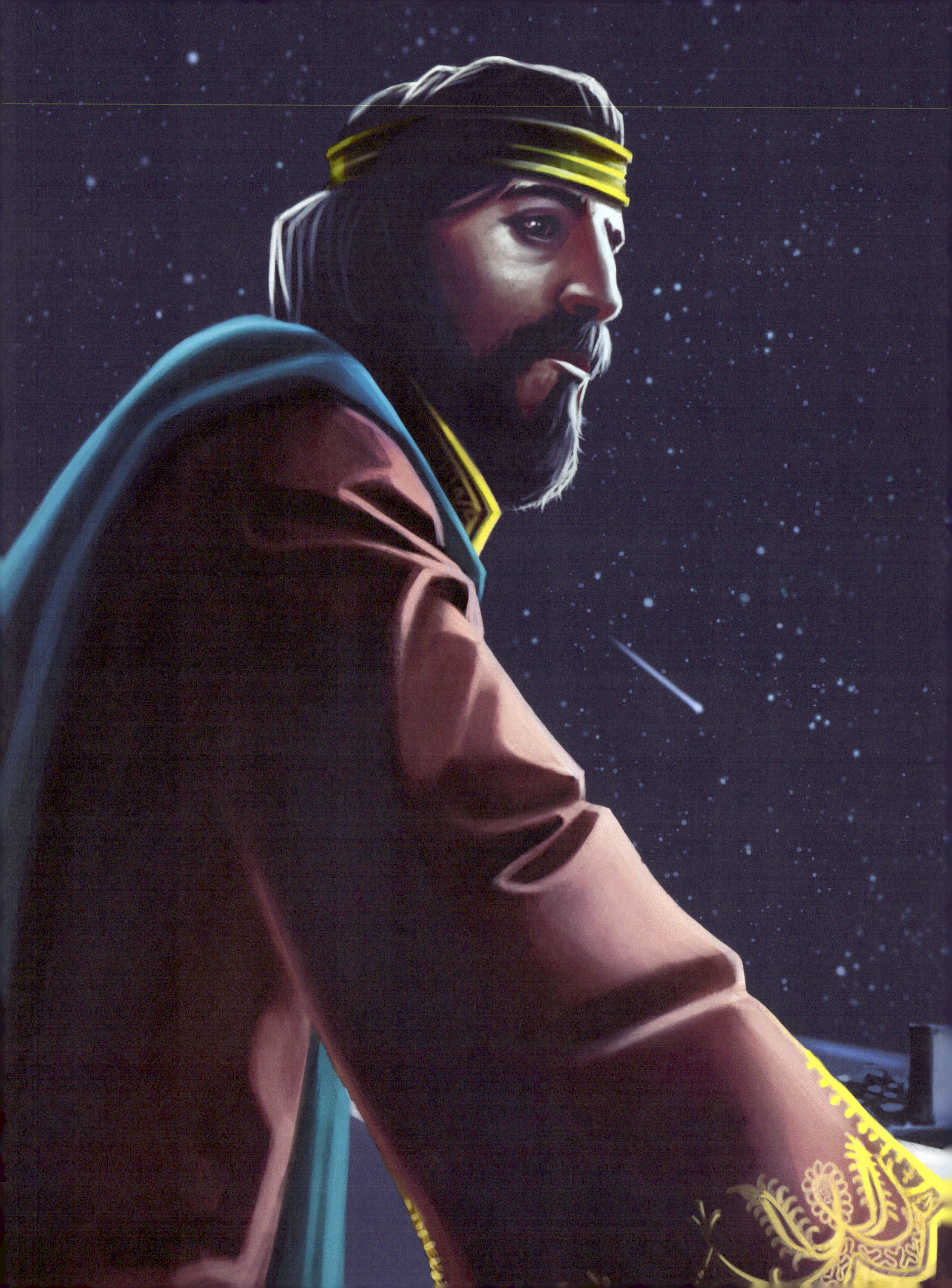

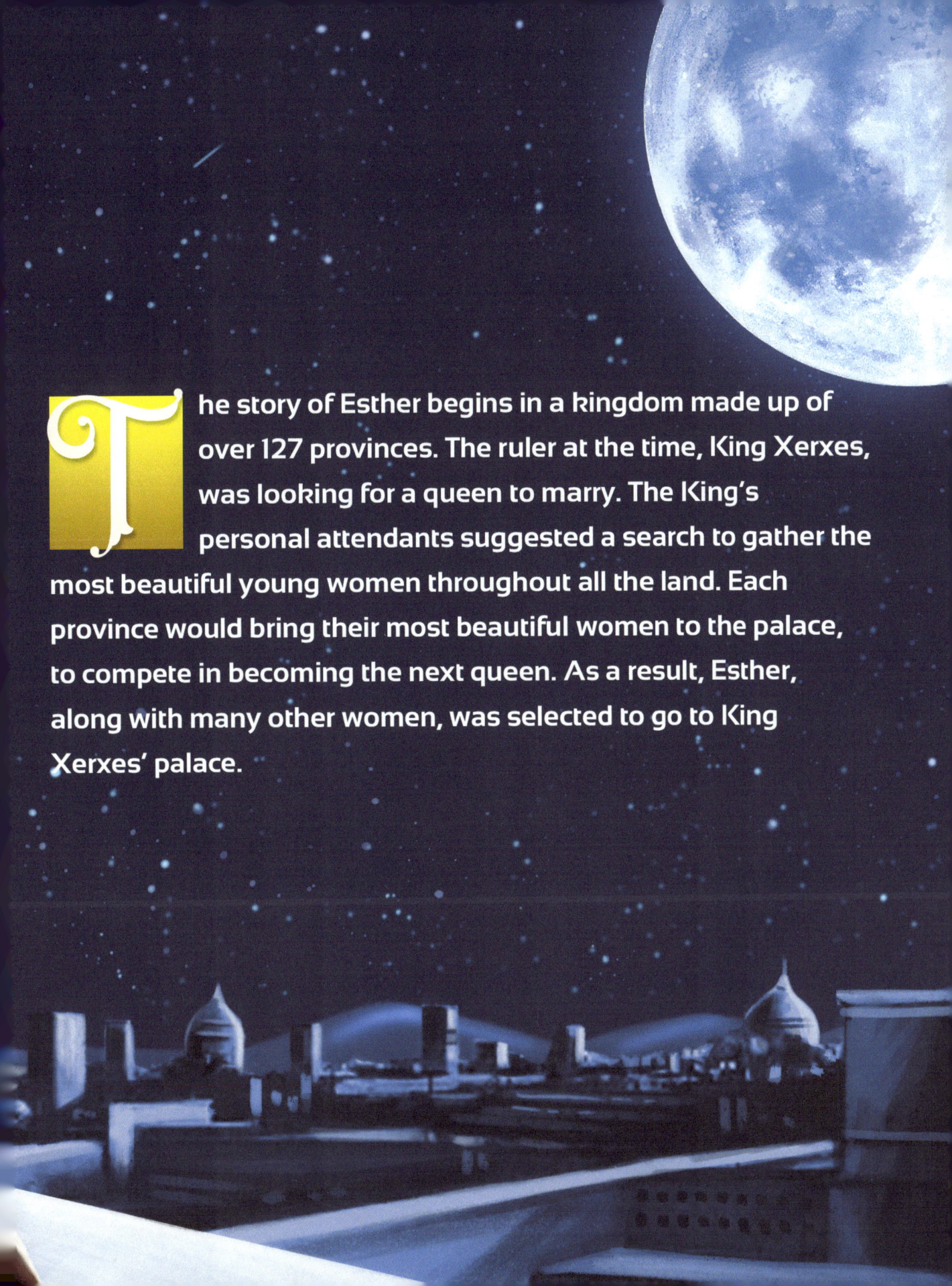

The story of Esther begins in a kingdom made up of over 127 provinces. The ruler at the time, King Xerxes, was looking for a queen to marry. The King's personal attendants suggested a search to gather the most beautiful young women throughout all the land. Each province would bring their most beautiful women to the palace, to compete in becoming the next queen. As a result, Esther, along with many other women, was selected to go to King Xerxes' palace.

"Don't tell them where you're from," advised Esther's cousin Mordecai "You'll understand some day!" They quickly whisked Esther away into the King's palace. There, she and many other women began their transformation to become the next queen.

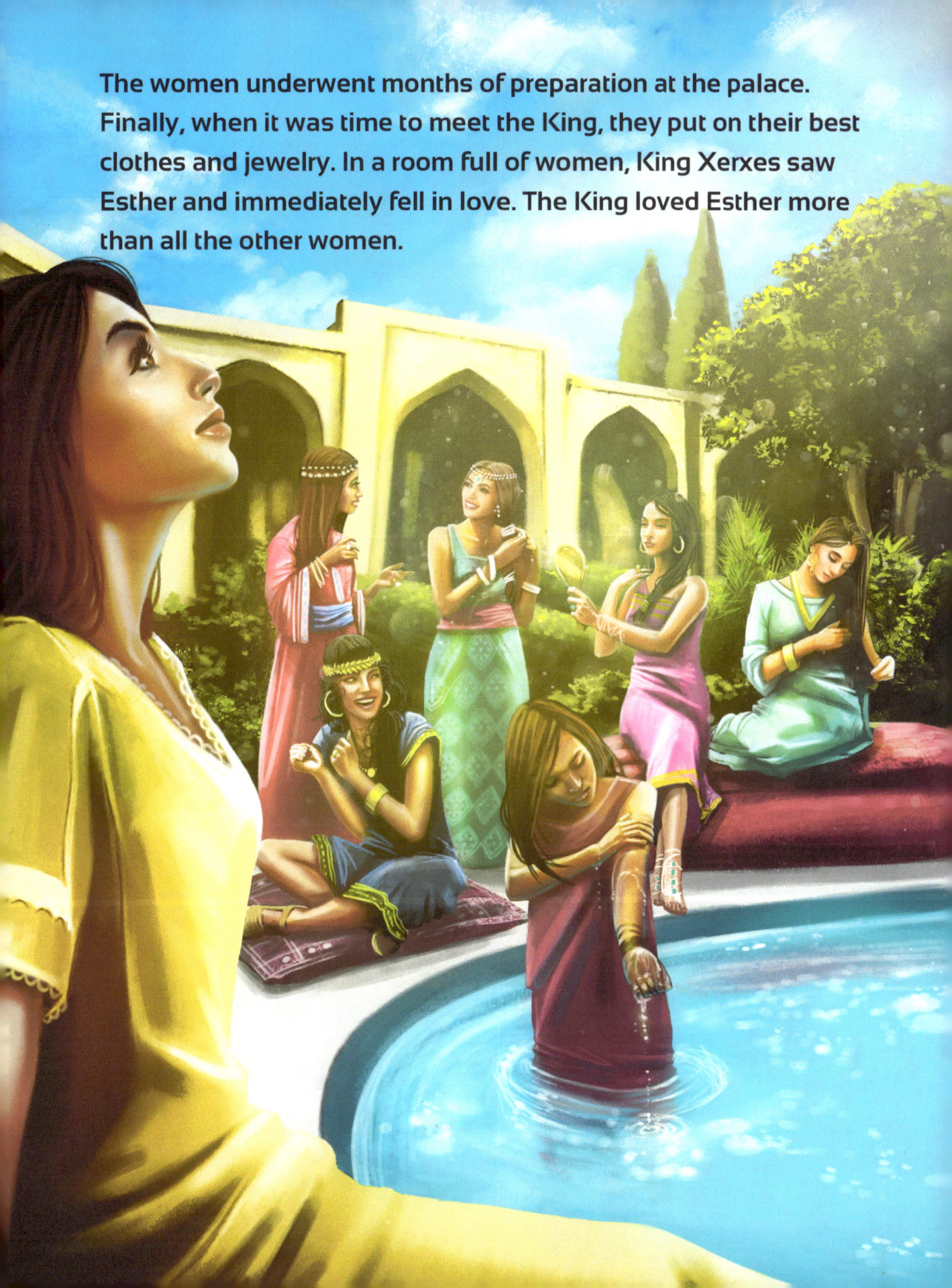

The women underwent months of preparation at the palace. Finally, when it was time to meet the King, they put on their best clothes and jewelry. In a room full of women, King Xerxes saw Esther and immediately fell in love. The King loved Esther more than all the other women.

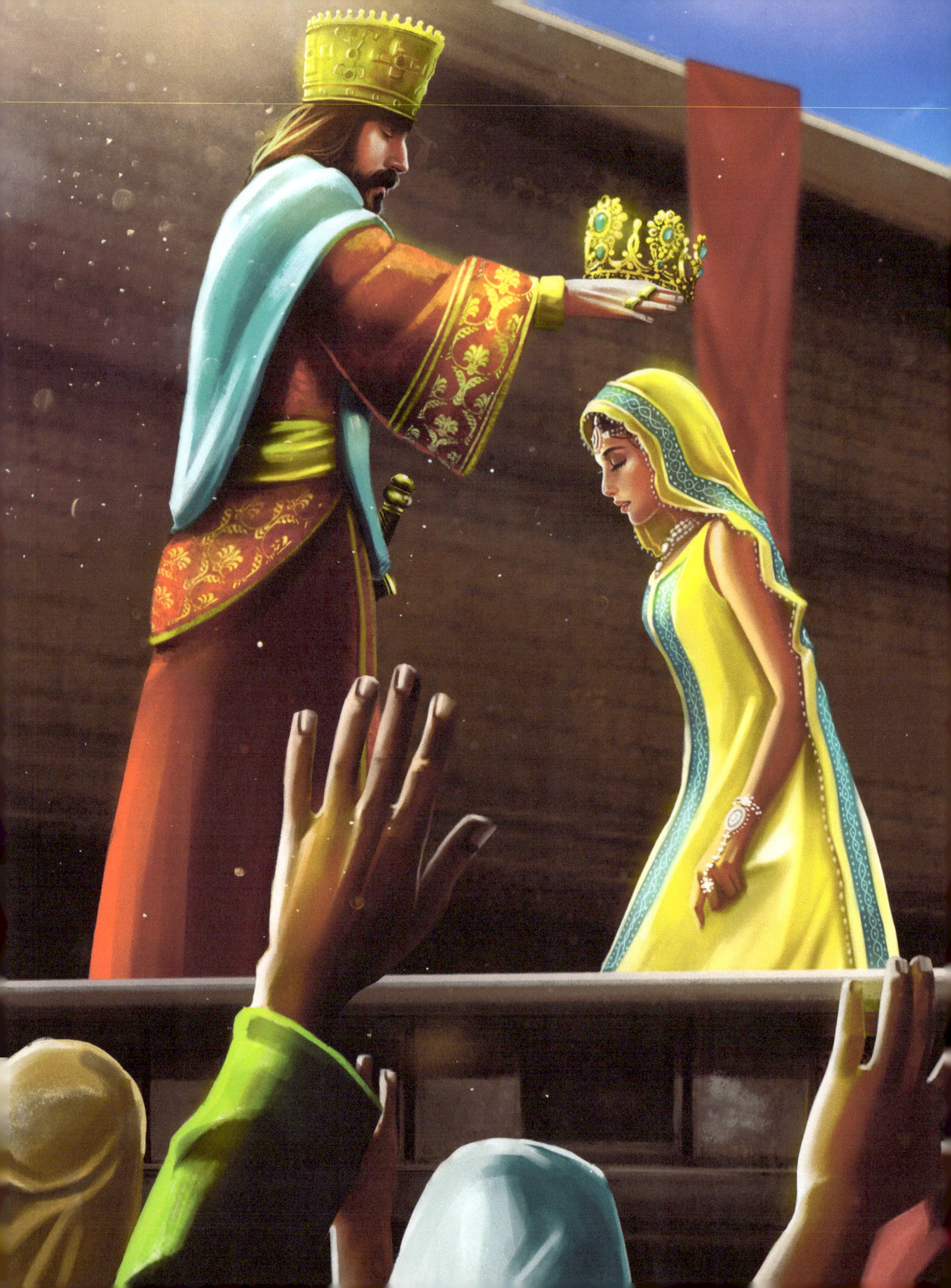

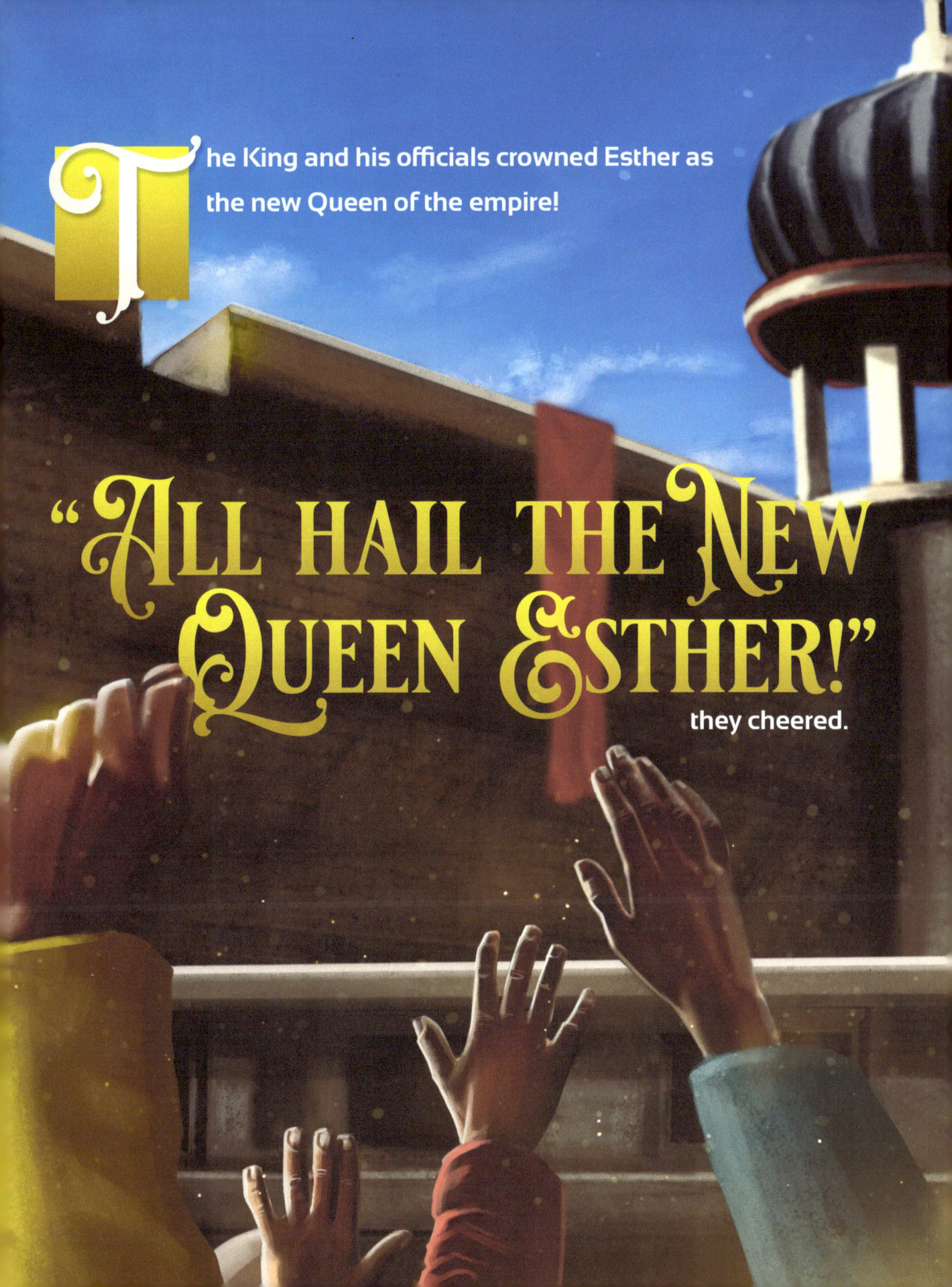

The King and his officials crowned Esther as the new Queen of the empire!

"All hail the New Queen Esther!" they cheered.

One day Esther's cousin Mordecai was on duty at the King's gate. There, he overheard two palace guards plotting to kill the King. Mordecai told Queen Esther about what he had heard. She immediately shared this information with the palace officials and they discovered it to be true! All credit was given to Mordecai for stopping the plot against King Xerxes. It was also recorded in the King's book of history.

Sometime later, King Xerxes promoted a man by the name of Haman to be second in command. A decree was made for everyone to bow before Haman as a sign of respect and honor. As he traveled back to the palace the people bowed before Haman, with the exception of Mordecai! Haman was furious!

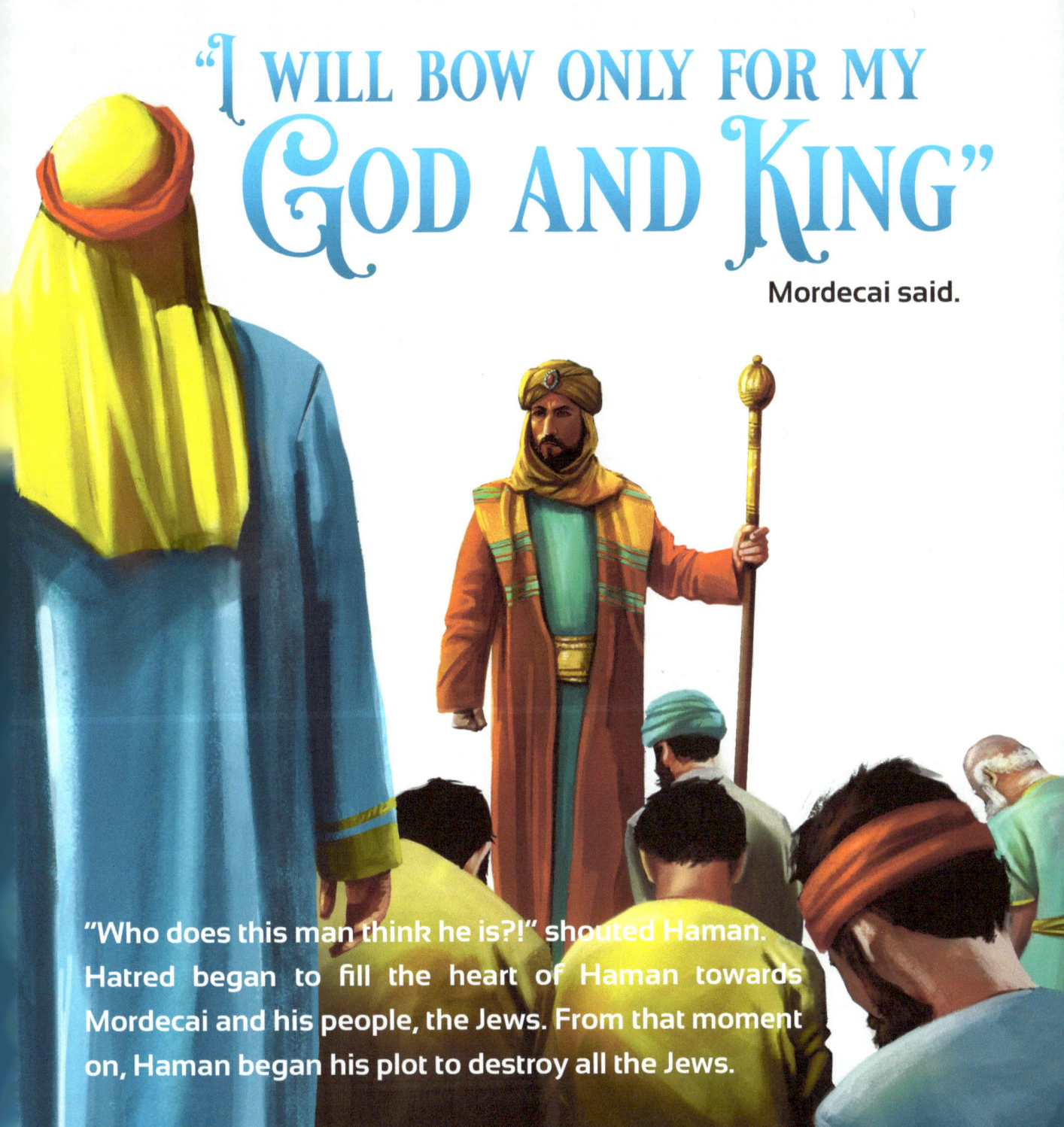

"I WILL BOW ONLY FOR MY GOD AND KING"

Mordecai said.

"Who does this man think he is?!" shouted Haman. Hatred began to fill the heart of Haman towards Mordecai and his people, the Jews. From that moment on, Haman began his plot to destroy all the Jews.

Months went by and evil Haman took his plans to destroy the Jews to King Xerxes. "I only have your best interest in mind, my great King" he explained. "These people do not obey the King's orders and decrees. They are different than us, strangers in this land!" Haman continued. "They're a threat to this kingdom and should be dealt with immediately."

"What should be done?" asked a concerned King Xerxes. Haman said, "If it pleases the King, let a decree be written:

THAT THEY ALL BE DESTROYED!"

So the King took off his signet ring and gave it to Haman, enemy of the Jews.

"Do what seems good to you."

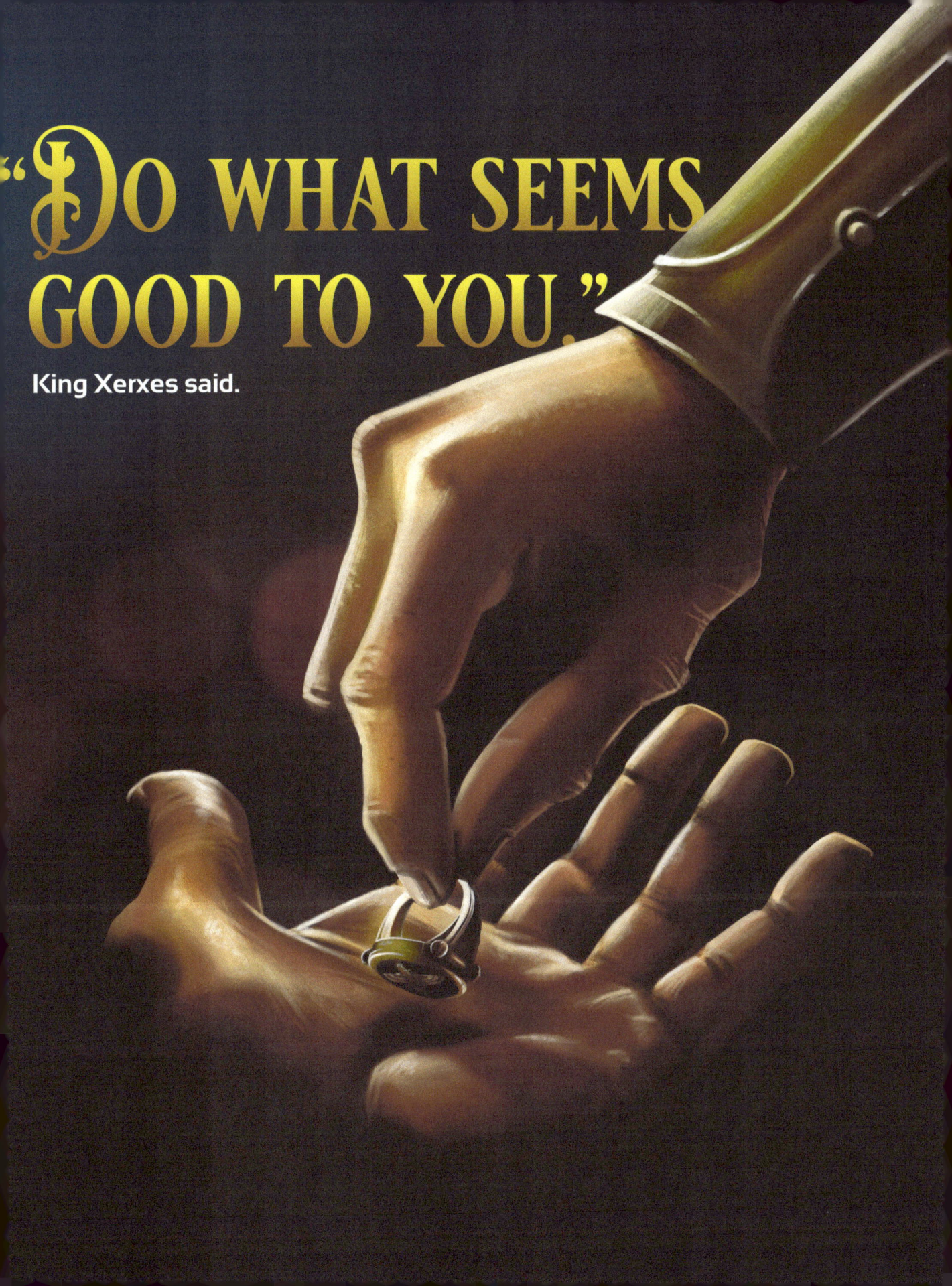

King Xerxes said.

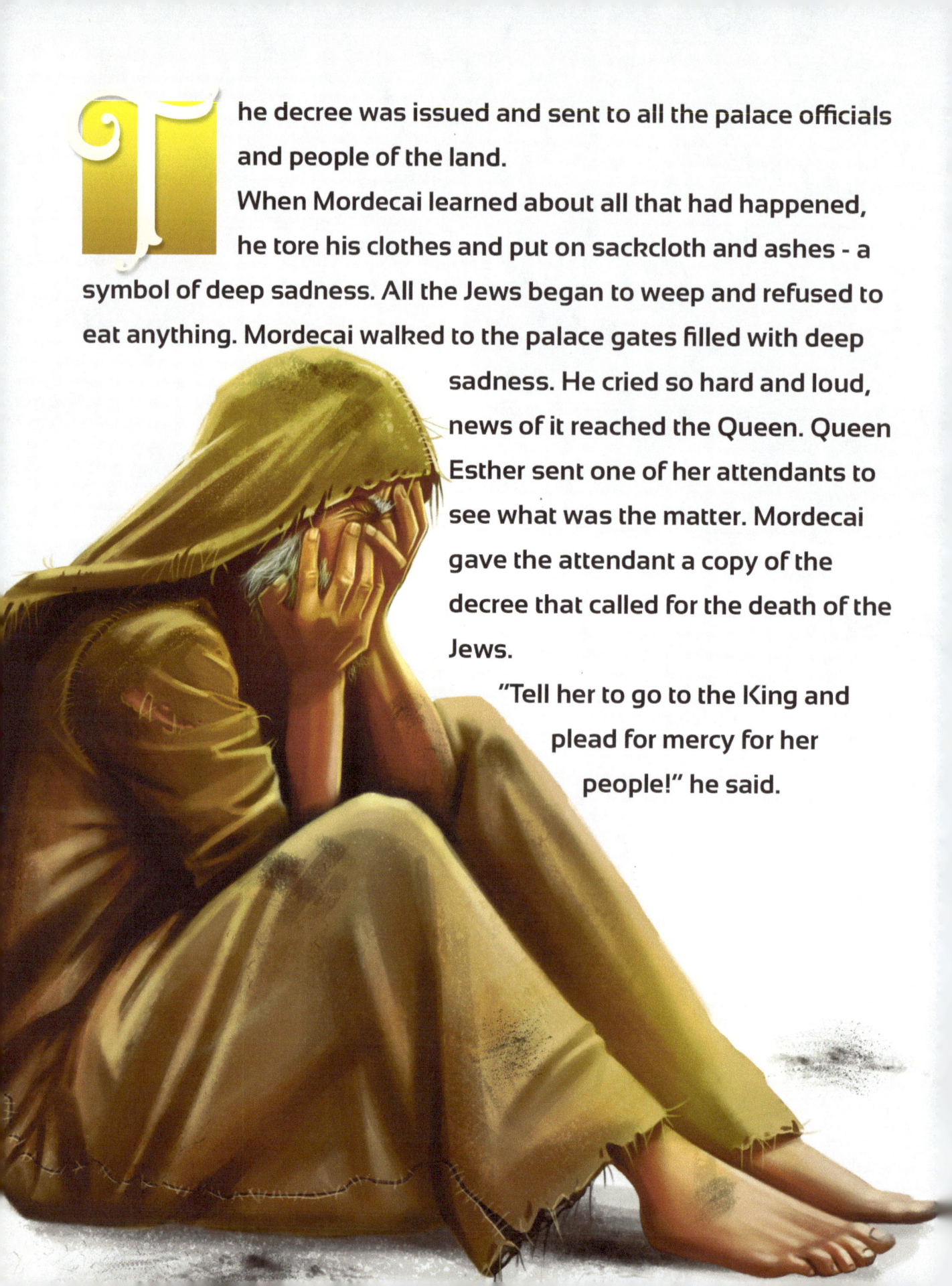

The decree was issued and sent to all the palace officials and people of the land.

When Mordecai learned about all that had happened, he tore his clothes and put on sackcloth and ashes - a symbol of deep sadness. All the Jews began to weep and refused to eat anything. Mordecai walked to the palace gates filled with deep sadness. He cried so hard and loud, news of it reached the Queen. Queen Esther sent one of her attendants to see what was the matter. Mordecai gave the attendant a copy of the decree that called for the death of the Jews.

"Tell her to go to the King and plead for mercy for her people!" he said.

The attendant returned to Esther with Mordecai's message. Then, Queen Esther told the attendant to send Mordecai her reply: "All the King's officials and people everywhere know what happens when someone stands before the King without being invited. They are doomed for death unless the King holds out his gold scepter. And the King hasn't invited me to come in 30 days!"

Mordecai replied, "If you keep quiet, deliverance for us will come from another place, but you and all your family will die. Who knows if God has chosen you

FOR SUCH A TIME AS THIS?!"

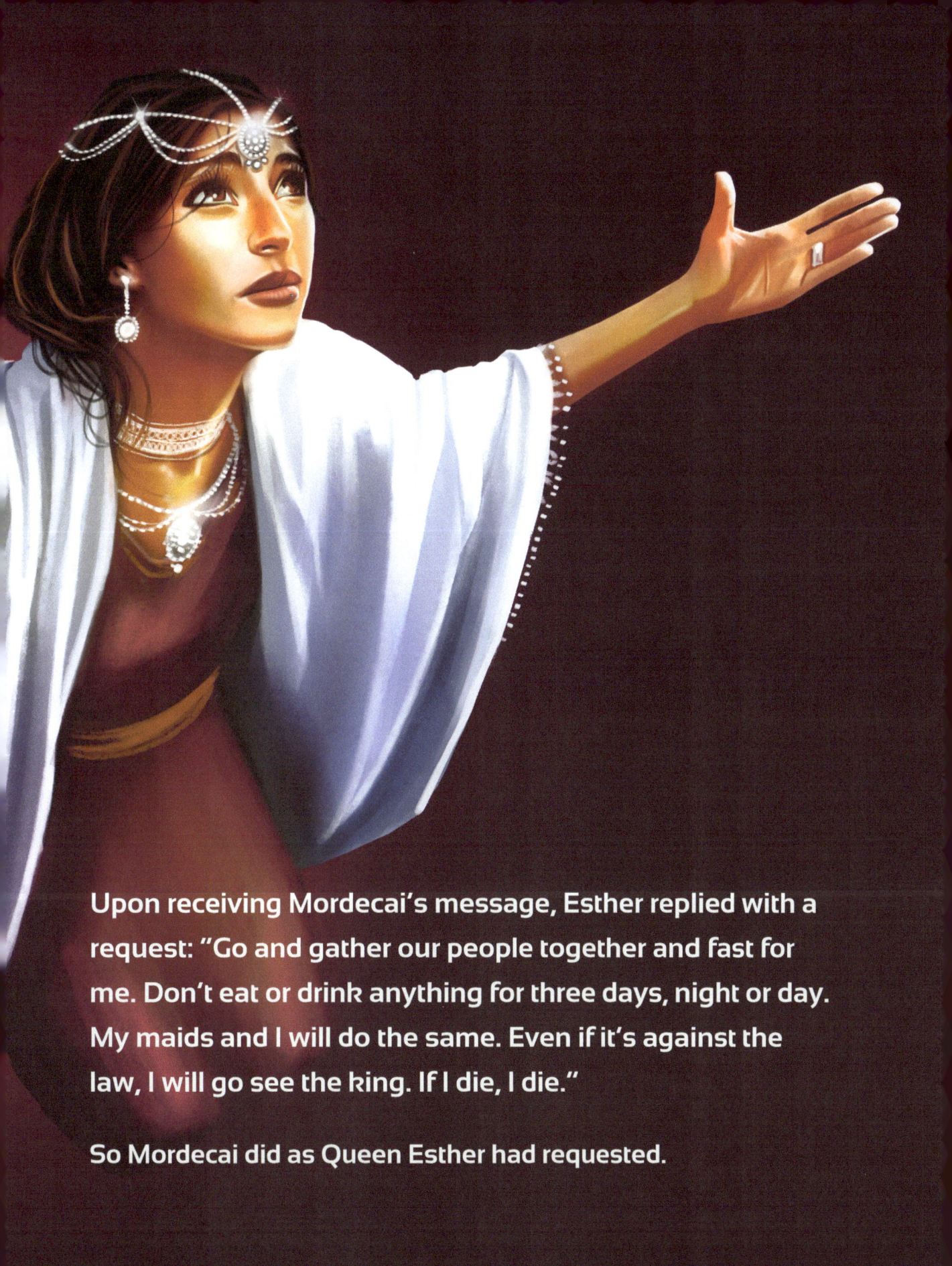

Upon receiving Mordecai's message, Esther replied with a request: "Go and gather our people together and fast for me. Don't eat or drink anything for three days, night or day. My maids and I will do the same. Even if it's against the law, I will go see the king. If I die, I die."

So Mordecai did as Queen Esther had requested.

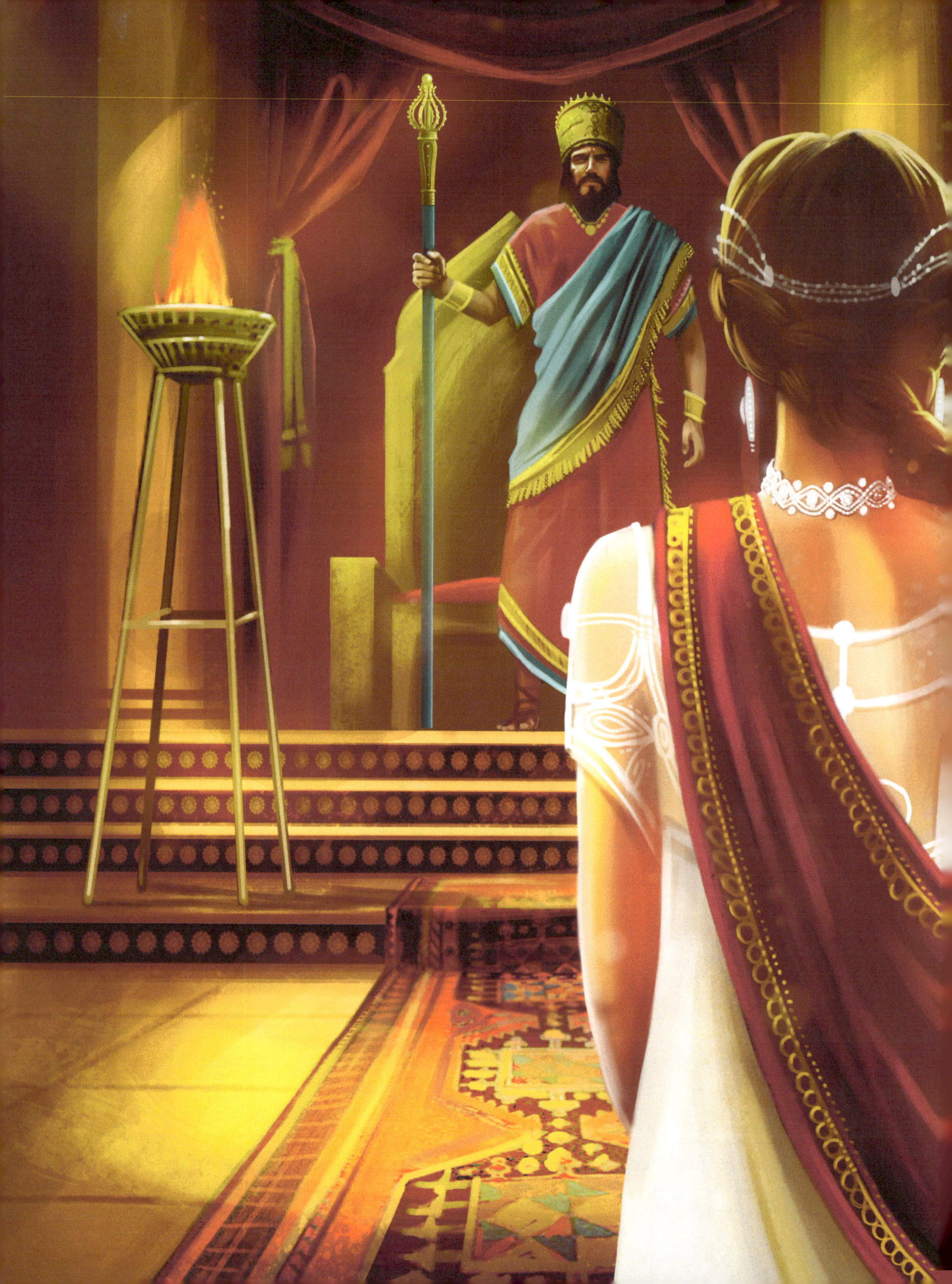

On the third day of the fast, Queen Esther put on her royal clothing and entered the inner court of the palace uninvited. The King was sitting on his royal throne and saw Queen Esther standing there. Instead of sending her to her death,

HE WELCOMED HER AND REACHED OUT HIS GOLDEN SCEPTER.

"What do you want Queen Esther? I'll give you whatever you ask for, even if it's half of the kingdom!" King Xerxes exclaimed.

Queen Esther replied, "If it pleases the King, I would like to invite you and Haman to attend a banquet I've prepared for you tonight."

So the King and Haman went to the banquet that night.

At the banquet King Xerxes turned to the Queen and asked, "Now, what is it that you really want? What is your request? I'll give you anything you want even if it's half the kingdom!"

"If it pleases the King" Queen Esther responded, "come back to another banquet I've prepared for you and Haman tomorrow. Then I will finally tell you what this is all about."

That night Haman excitedly hurried home to tell his wife about the wonderful banquet Queen Esther had given. He saw Mordecai at the king's gate and noticed Mordecai didn't bow or show fear at his presence. He was filled with anger against Mordecai and hurried home.

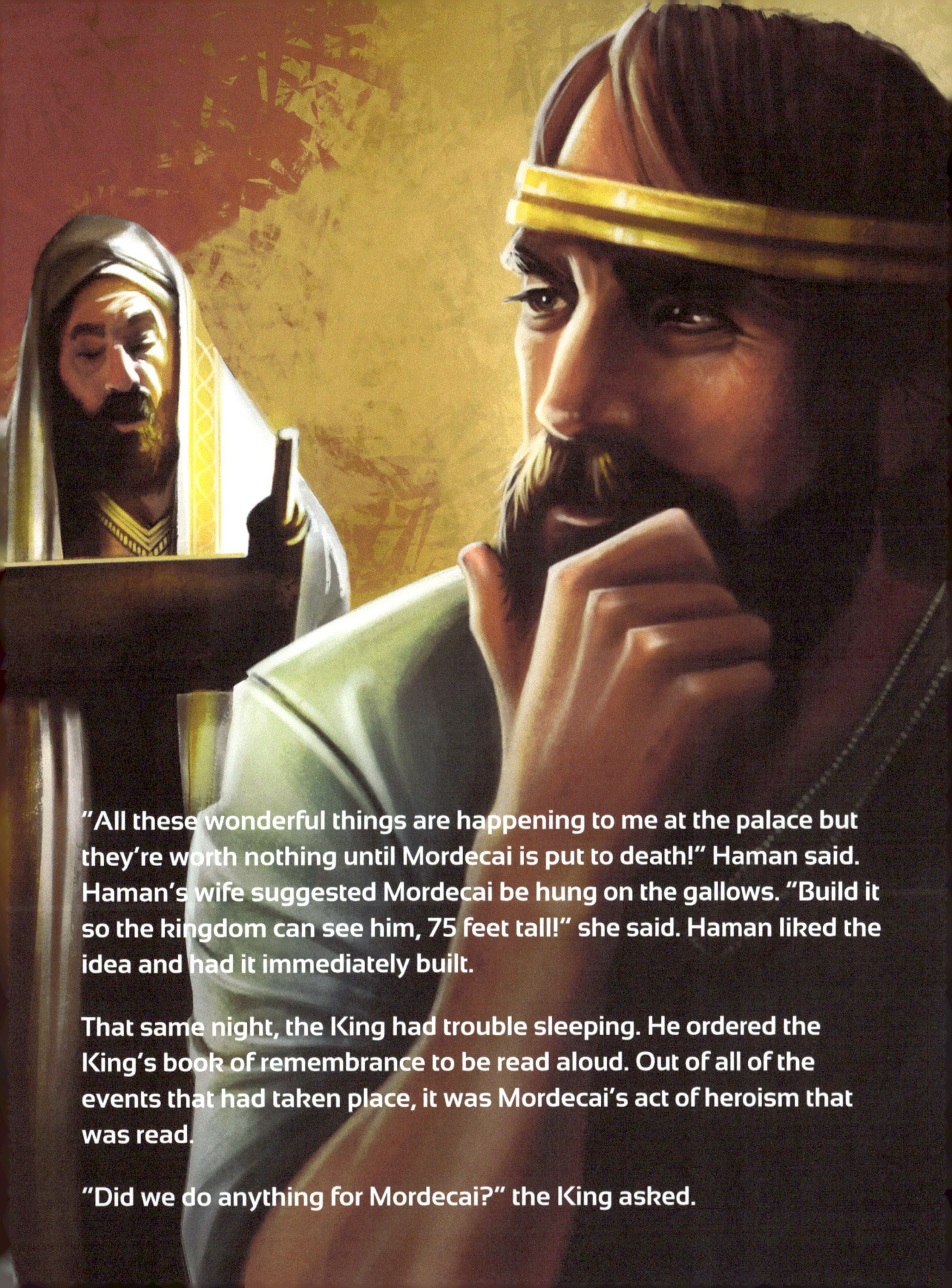

"All these wonderful things are happening to me at the palace but they're worth nothing until Mordecai is put to death!" Haman said. Haman's wife suggested Mordecai be hung on the gallows. "Build it so the kingdom can see him, 75 feet tall!" she said. Haman liked the idea and had it immediately built.

That same night, the King had trouble sleeping. He ordered the King's book of remembrance to be read aloud. Out of all of the events that had taken place, it was Mordecai's act of heroism that was read.

"Did we do anything for Mordecai?" the King asked.

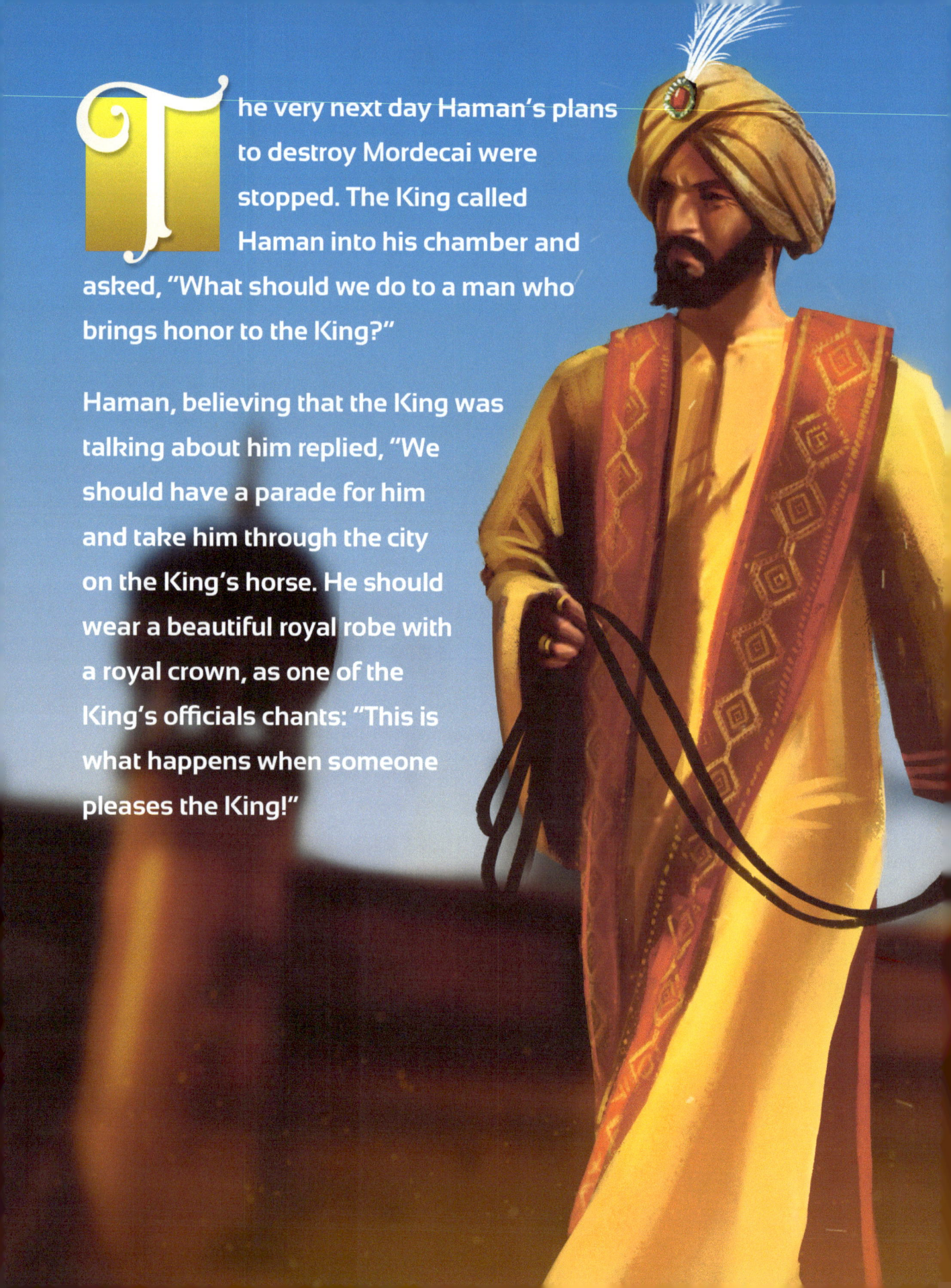

The very next day Haman's plans to destroy Mordecai were stopped. The King called Haman into his chamber and asked, "What should we do to a man who brings honor to the King?"

Haman, believing that the King was talking about him replied, "We should have a parade for him and take him through the city on the King's horse. He should wear a beautiful royal robe with a royal crown, as one of the King's officials chants: "This is what happens when someone pleases the King!"

"Wonderful idea Haman!" King Xerxes exclaimed. "Do this for our hero Mordecai."

During Queen Esther's second banquet, the King, Queen Esther and Haman were all present. They were sitting around the banquet table when King Xerxes asked, "Tell me what you really want, my Queen. Whatever you want I'll give you, even half of the kingdom!"

Esther replied, "If it pleases the King, I ask that you would spare my life and the lives of my people. A decree was issued for the death of all the Jews!"

"Who would dare touch the Queen?! Who's responsible for such a wicked thing?!" King Xerxes cried out furiously.

"The Evil Haman!"

Esther pointed towards a very shocked Haman.
"What do you have to say for yourself?!" the King roared.
"I don't know what she's talking about!" Haman exclaimed.
King Xerxes jumped to his feet in rage.

One of the King's officials spoke up and said "Haman built a 75 foot gallow for his enemy Mordecai."

"Hang Him On It!"

the King yelled.

On that same day the decree to kill every Jew was reversed and they were given the right to unite to defend their lives.

Great joy filled the city and

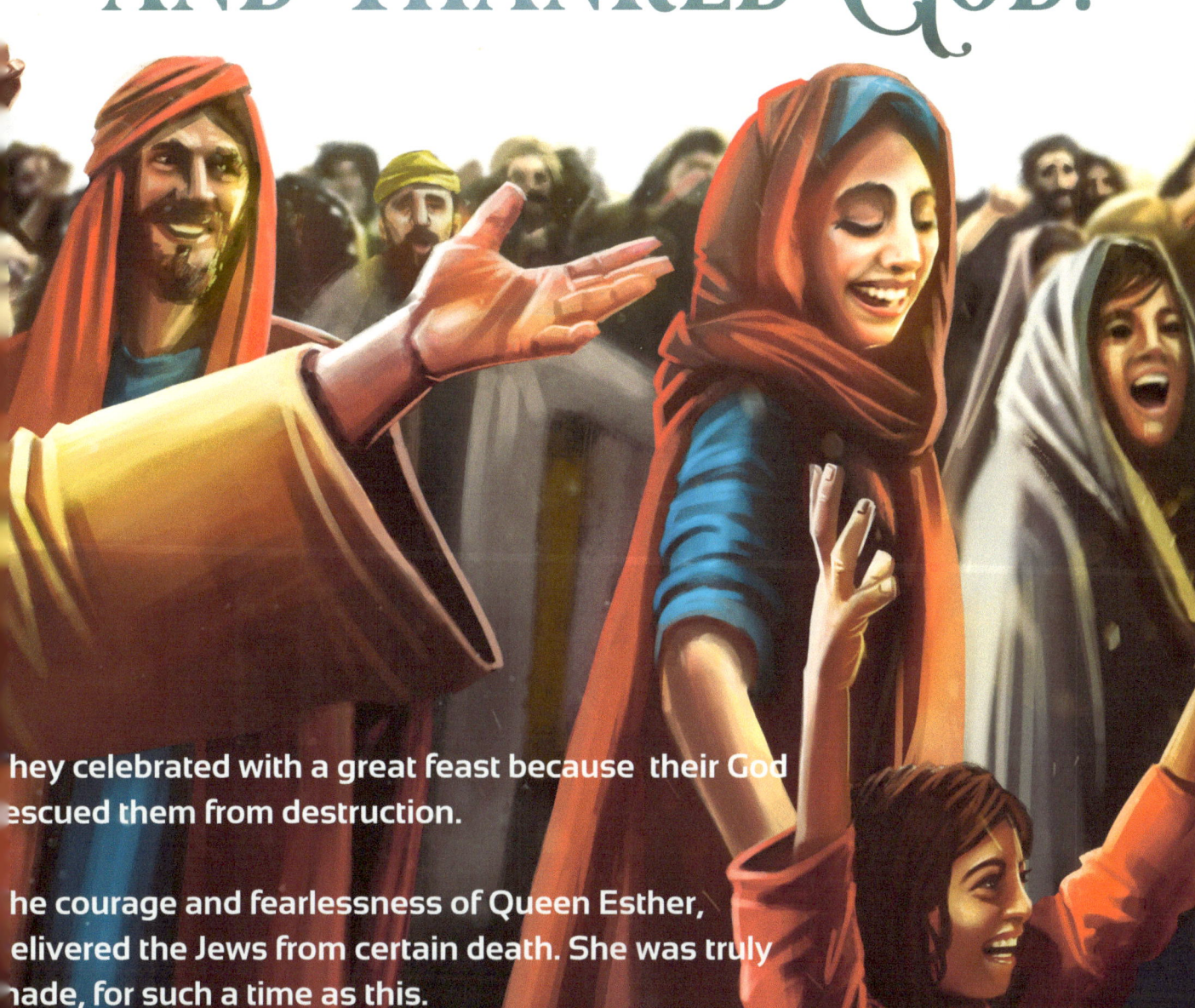

The Jews rejoiced and thanked God.

hey celebrated with a great feast because their God
escued them from destruction.

he courage and fearlessness of Queen Esther,
elivered the Jews from certain death. She was truly
ade, for such a time as this.